MW00427705

Penguins, Pain
and the
Whole Shebang

To Matt & Krystal —
Here's to listening to God!

Penguins, Pain
and the
Whole Shebang

Why I Do the Things I Do

By God

as told to
John Shore

[signature] 12/10/05

SEABURY BOOKS
an imprint of
CHURCH PUBLISHING, NEW YORK

ISBN 1-59627-019-5

Seabury Books
Church Publishing Inc.
445 Fifth Avenue
New York, NY 10016
www.churchpublishing.org

5 4 3 2 1

To you, the reader.
And to all other humans.
Well, to all mammals. And birds, too.
And fish—we can't forget the fish.
Okay: to every single living entity
or physical form that ever has spent,
or ever will spend, one moment on earth.

Also, to John's wife, Catherine.
How she does what she does is anyone's guess.

Contents

OPENING PART   9

THE CONVERSATION JOHN OVERHEARD   15

    But Wait! There's More   35

BEING OBJECTIONABLE   37

    I just don't believe in God, period.   40

    If you really exist, why don't you prove it?   49

    What's the deal with evil, anyway?   59

    Why are so many Christians so obnoxious?   69

    What's that whole "Atonement" thing
    actually *mean?*   79

    Isn't it enough that I believe in God?   84

Contents _____

What's the deal about God actually writing
the Bible?   89

Even if I do believe in Christ, do I really have to
go to church every Sunday?   105

So how would being a Christian actually
improve my life?   110

AFTERWORD by John Shore   115

ACKNOWLEDGMENTS   128

OPENING PART

Hi, there. I'm God—the Christian God, to be precise.

No, really. It's me. I'm not kidding.

Hey, I can write. I've written before. As you know. As *everyone* knows.

Though of course it's true that this is hardly my usual means of communicating. I definitely prefer a much more ... intimate approach. This is something you also know— whether you *think* you know it or not.

Which is a whole other topic of conversation.

Anyway, I'm now sitting here in the early morning light, typing these words onto a computer screen. (Typing! Computers! What *will* you people think up next? I shudder to imagine!) The reason I'm doing this began about three minutes ago, when I noticed that the fellow whose body and mind I'm now occupying, John Shore

(*Hello! John here! Hi!*), had leapt out of bed, and veritably dashed to his computer.

Now John is not a man prone to dashing anywhere — and certainly not upon waking; on most days I can barely get the boy to *move* until about noon. And yet there he was, before he'd even had his morning cup of whatever it is he's currently drinking in his never-ending quest to have it not be coffee, typing with such fervor that for a moment I actually found myself wishing that I'd given him a few extra fingers.

Because I'm invariably interested whenever any human being gets excited about anything (especially if it involves anything new to them — and *especially* if it involves any sort of creative act), I came up behind John, and looked over his shoulder to see what he was writing.

And I saw that what he was writing was a little two-person play.

And I saw that one of the characters in that play was I — and that the other was the angel Michael, whom I am sometimes pleased to call Mickey.

And (believe me) it didn't take me long at all to realize that John was typing what amounted to the transcript of

10

an _actual, private conversation_ Mickey and I once had a very long time ago.

Try to imagine my surprise.

For verily is that just so very, very wrong.

It's also not the kind of thing that's anywhere near as rare as it should be. Turns out it's a lot more complicated than you'd think to construct and keep perfectly foolproof a three-dimensional universe in which fully independent, fully _conscious_ beings wander around doing all kinds of things, like...well, like sleeping, for one.

Sleeping. What an intense, complicated design feature _that_ turned out to be. You just wouldn't _believe_ some of the things you people do, see, and think when you're asleep.

The key word, of course, being "asleep." As in "not awake."

As in Totally Unique and Separate Form of Consciousness.

The bottom line? What happens in Dreamland is supposed to _stay_ in Dreamland.

That said, what happened last night isn't supposed to happen under _any_ circumstances. But, alas, it did: What amounts to the consciousness of our little Curious John

11

ended up wandering into a place it wasn't supposed to be, and seeing a (hmmm...how to put this?) *replay* of something it wasn't supposed to see—or that at the very least John wasn't supposed to *remember* seeing the next morning.

Wrong, wrong, wrong.

Well, whaddaya gonna do? Stuff happens.

But here's the thing: The conversation John's Essence inadvertently came upon happened to be a truly key one in the development of Youse Peoples. And as I watched John typing what he could remember of that interaction, I saw that he was here and there getting a word of it wrong. Which isn't that big a deal—it's not like he's a *stenographer* or anything—but it did occur to me that if just about any conversation I've ever had should be preserved for posterity (um...any that I didn't actually have on *earth,* that is), it's probably this one.

So, suddenly inspired to Get It Right, I moved in, and went Eminent Domain on John's glutes.

And now here I am inside of John, controlling his arms and legs and thoughts, and generally just being... well, him!

Corporeal existence is suuuuuuuuch a trip.

But look who I'm telling!

Gravity. It's so...amazingly innovative—if I do say so myself.

Speaking of major innovations that absolutely define life for humans on earth, please allow me to now present to you the following verbatim re-creation of an Actual, Heavenly Duo Confab, courtesy of the interactively coordinated team of John Shore and me, the original Mr. Big. (Though, let's face it, in any working relationship it's always more efficient to have one person functioning as the Supreme Commander—and you can trust that John feels entirely comfortable with me in that role.)

And here we go:

THE CONVERSATION
JOHN OVERHEARD

(The royal purple curtain goes up, and we see ME in my wonderful, cozy, best-place-ever workshop, busily putting the final touches on my prototype for the human being. Enter one of my all-time favorite angels, the ever-loyal MICKEY.)

Mickey: Wassup, Lord of Lords? Just thought I'd pop in and—whoa! What is *that?*

Me: You like it?

Mickey: I *love* it! What is it?

Me: I'm calling it the "Human Being."

15

Mickey: The "Human Being," huh? Wow. Looks like Your Holy Omnipotence has done it again!

Me: Oh, stop. But thank you.

Mickey: I'm serious. Creator of All or not, this...this is *something!* What's it do?

Me: A *lot!* It moves; it processes all kinds of information at truly stunning rates; it *fully* communicates; it's got state-of-the-art ocular and aural capabilities...and get this: It *stays* upright like that!

Mickey: No. Way.

Me: Way! It does! It self-locomotes in this exact position—and I mean, this baby can really *move.* And while it's moving, it stays upright on those two flat parts on the ground!

Mickey: Unbelievable. I feel like falling over just looking at it. It's so *tall!*

Me: And look at this doohickey right here.

Mickey: What is that?

_Me:_ I call it a thumb. See? It's opposable.

Mickey: An opposable thumb! Amazing! Um...what's an opposable thumb?

_Me:_ It is one serious design innovation, is what. See how it works in opposition to these other protrusions right here? See that? Do you know what that means?

Mickey: Wait, don't tell me. Um...lemme think...that it can fly?

_Me:_ No, not that it can _fly_. They're not stubby little _wings_.

Mickey: Well, maybe if they spun real fast, they could...

_Me:_ No, no, they don't _spin_. They make it so the human can _hold_ things! Manipulate objects! Maneuver any thing, of basically any size, in whatever way it pleases. And it gives him a grip you practically need lightning to loosen.

Mickey: Oh, I see! Excellent! Well, it looks like you've done it again, O Glorious One. Um, what's this weird looking thing here?

_Me:_ That's his procreation apparatus.

Mickey: Really? That?

Me: Yes, that. Why?

Mickey: Is it still in development?

Me: Yeah—I'm working on making it *spin* fast enough for flight. Between it and the roto-thumbs, my new human-copter is almost ready to launch.

Mickey: If I didn't know you better, I'd think you're being sarcastic.

Me: [*laughing*] Ha! You crack me up! And you're right: The thing is pretty bizarre looking.

Mickey: But what do I know? I'm just an adoring minion— and one who can barely keep his harp tuned at that. It seems okay to me. As long as it gets the job done, I guess.

Me: Yeah, it definitely works. Well, maybe I'll try covering it with some hair or something.

Mickey: There you go. But overall, the Human Being's pretty much done, right? I mean, it sure *looks* ready to go.

Me: It is. I've just got a few adjustments left to make. I keep tinkering with it. Like, I'm a little concerned with these things here—what I call the "teeth." See 'em? I'm not sure I've got the whole pain-to-durability ratio quite right here.

Mickey: "Pain," Lord?

Me: Oh, it's a self-contained feedback system I've installed in the human to make it aware of when some part of it's been damaged. I want whatever part's been harmed to relay a message to that effect back to the human's brain, so that he'll know if his neck is twisted too far around, or if his nose fell off, or whatever. Stuff like that's gonna *hurt.* But at the same time, I don't want it to hurt *too* much, or too soon: I don't want all the humans just *standing* there, because they're afraid to move. So I'm trying to get that whole system properly calibrated. It's the same thing that's got me a little worried about this whole area right here.

Mickey: What is that?

Me: I call it the "shin bone." I should probably dink with it some more. On the other hand, I'm so anxious to spark this bad boy to life, I might send it out just like it is!

Mickey: Do it! But where are you sending it to?

Me: Well, I'm going to put him—and a female version of him you absolutely will not *believe* — down on that new planet I just made, the green and blue one.

Mickey: You mean the one that's got all that amazing, clear, gloopy kind of stuff that makes your hair go all—

Me: Yeah, that's it—the one with *water* on it.

Mickey: I *love* that stuff!

Me: I know! So do I! I can't believe the way it came out! Entirely beneficial—yet corrosive!

Mickey: How do you do it?

Me: I'm telling you, if I wasn't God, I'd have no idea.

Mickey: Did you make that planet just for the humans? I know how you like to give all your creatures their own special place.

Me: I do. And I did. That planet's just for them.

Mickey: They're gonna *love* it down there!

Me: There'll be a lot down there to love, that's for sure. They're also going to have a lot to struggle with, though.

Mickey: They are? Struggle? What's "struggle," Lord?

Me: It's where things aren't absolutely perfect all the time.

Mickey: I'm sorry. You're losing me.

Me: Look—you love your life, right?

Mickey: Yes! Always! Praise be to you, Lord!

Me: And why do you love your life so much?

Mickey: Because I am always in your presence!

Me: Right. But what if it wasn't like that? What if it wasn't always as easy for you to experience me as it is for you right now?

Mickey: I don't understand, Lord. Is it something I've said? Something I've done? That sour note I hit during our harp concert the other night? Sure, at the time we all thought it was funny, but I could see how later on, you might....

Me: Oh, stop it, you goof. I'm not talking about you. I'm talking about the humans. They're going to exist in a system defined by undeviating rules about space and time that will have the effect of essentially *hiding* me from them. And I'm going to give them all an absolute free will, too. That combination will incline them toward an independence that's truly unprecedented.

Mickey: Really? But all of us up here have free will, Father. And we all love you.

Me: Yeah, Mickey, but one of the reasons you do is because the vibrant immediacy of our co-relationship makes it fundamentally *easier* for you to love me. I mean, I'm right *here.*

Mickey: But you're everywhere, my Lord. Where are you not?

Me: Well, that's what I'm saying: I'm going to put the humans into a system designed in such a way as to make

22

it perfectly reasonable for them to wonder if I'm really _anywhere_. Their realm of experience will be so rigidly physical that it will be a challenge for them to believe in anything that doesn't register with the five senses they'll be equipped with.

Mickey: The five whatses?

_Me:_ Senses. It's a way of breaking up their experience into something like different, simultaneously broadcasting channels. You see, Mick, you experience your reality as a constant whole, as a kind of infinitely dimensional gestalt, in which your personal identity isn't in any way... well, you know what your life is like.

Mickey: Glorious! Infinitely rewarding! Praise be to you, the source of all joy!

_Me:_ You're too kind. But the point is, you _naturally_ understand your consciousness as an extension of my own. So it's hard, if not impossible, for you to grasp the way in which humans will experience me, and their reality. They're going to exist in a system that precludes their knowing me with the same kind of logical, physical

23

surety that will characterize almost all the rest of their knowledge. They'll very much tend to trust only what they can see, feel, hear, touch, and smell. And they won't be able to do *any* of that with me. In a very real way, I'm going to remain hidden from them.

Mickey: For the life of me I can't imagine a world in which you're not always just...*there.*

Me: And you'd be amazed at what I had to do with space and time in order to make it seem as if I'm not. I've created an entire universe for the humans in which they're both very nearly *fixed.*

Mickey: No!

Me: Yes! I've done this whole linear thing with time that I'm actually quite excited about. It turns out time's a really *fun* medium to work with! I've reconfigured it into all of these interconnected units of perception, see, and then sort of flattened and stretched them all out, so that in purely physical terms the human won't be able to experience time as anything but a kind of seamless procession of sequential experiences. I've also fixed *matter* in a way you would not believe. I've taken its essence from our world here, and woven it into the humans' world in a way that allows it to take on a truly infinite array of forms, so that in the perceptual context of the three-dimensional world in which the human exists, it will....

Mickey: Whoa. Did you say *three*-dimensional?

Me: Yes! Didn't I mention that? There's only going to be three dimensions in the humans' world!

Mickey: No way.

Me: Three! That's it! They're going to think (at least for a very, very long time) that there's only three *anywhere!* You should see it! In the humans' world, forms of coordinating, inert, interdependent units of matter will take on a very real, distinct sort of objective independence. And these units will — or will certainly seem to — exist independently of anyone's awareness of them. They'll *freeze*, in whatever shape they're in, wherever they're placed. Just stay there! Like they aren't alive at all! It's a total first for me. I really have to be *aware* of it in order to keep it

25

going. I love it! Humans will actually be plagued with this problem called The Stubbing of the Toe.

Mickey: That whatting of the what?

Me: It's what happens when one of these doolie-dads right here collides with a matter form that's comprised of too much stationary mass to move in response. It just *stays* where it is! The *toe* has to give!

Mickey: You're kidding with all this, right?

Me: No! I'm telling you: This is how their life will be.

Mickey: And they're going to be okay with all this? With the time thing? With the *stubbing?*

Me: Well, they won't know any different. The human's entire experience will amount to a rigidly linear trajectory in which, fully autonomous and self-aware, his senses perfectly attuned to the context in which he operates, he will, from what will feel to him like the purest form of nothing, enter at one end of his life, move along the impenetrable time-space continuum in which he'll operate, and then exit at the other end of his life span into what, again, he won't ever be able to objectively verify as being anything other than yet more nothingness.

Mickey: Um...no offense or anything, Father, but that doesn't exactly sound like oodles of fun.

Me: Well, the human'll have fun or not, depending on a universe of specific, temporal conditions unique to his experience. But one thing his life will *always* seem to him is real. Lights, colors, sounds, textures, tastes, smells — the whole apparatus in which human consciousness comes enmeshed is *so* physical it's going to be all the average human can do not to just hump everything it sees.

Mickey: Excuse me, your Lordship. Did you say "hump"?

Me: Oh, yeah. It's a whole new thing. It's how the humans are going to procreate. You don't want to know. But trust me: The physical act of reproducing themselves is going to feel *spectacular* to humans. It's going to feel so good it's basically going to drive them all insane. In fact, I've had to tone down the woman's whole deal with that act, because I realized that if I give the male and female the

27

same degree of what in the past you've probably heard me refer to as "sex drive," then...well, then I might as well just stick with monkeys.

Mickey: Monkeys ! That's it! I *knew* you'd done something like this before!

Me: Sure. And you remember them. Not exactly polite society, right?

Mickey: No kidding. I've still got stains on one of my robes. They were such...good aims, actually. And they sure were direct about their needs.

Me: Yeah, not a lot of mystery with the monkeys. Well, I'm giving the humans a whole other *order* of sex drive. They're gonna make monkeys look like...well, like you guys! Like angels!

Mickey: No!

Me: Yes. As you may recall, monkeys can only do the procreation mambo during pretty limited, specific phases of their biological cycles. But humans are going to be able to have sex *all the time!*

Mickey: I'm scared, Lord.

Me: With reason! They'll basically be in heat twenty-four seven!

Mickey: Twenty-four...howzat?

Me: Oh, it's this whole cyclical, mechanistic repeating loop thing that's part of that time-flattening phenomenon I was talking about. Never mind. The point is, given their whole interactive sensory orientation, and their body's never-say-die imperative to get down, get funky, and get *laid*, these creatures are looking at one formidable set of challenges standing between them and seeing the Big Picture.

Mickey: Which is you.

Me: Which is me.

Mickey: You'll be hidden.

Me: Like an albino in a blizzard.

Mickey: Like a what in a what?

Me: Oh, it has to do with the different colors humans will come in. Never mind.

Mickey: They're gonna come in different *colors*?

Me: I'm thinking about it. Green. Purple. Chartreuse. Or maybe something less dramatic. Maybe just browns and whites. Something more subdued.

Mickey: No, no! Go with the bright colors! Like this one here. He looks *great* in this neon green.

Me: Well, I'm just a little concerned about big colors freaking humans out. I don't want them, like, grouping together by colors and *turning* on each other, or anything.

Mickey: Oh, I can't imagine they would do that.

Me: Probably not. Still, I might keep them all in the same family of colors, just in case. Humans will have so much to deal with, I don't want anyone's *color* becoming an issue. Might as well play it safe.

Mickey: It does sound like they'll have some real challenges. So, I'm sorry: *Why* are you hiding yourself from them again?

Me: Because I don't want to interfere with their sense of independence—with the integrity of their free will.

Mickey: Because...?

Me: Because I want them to *choose* to love me.

Mickey: Right. Because that's more rewarding for you.

Me: And for them, too. Constantly choosing to love someone keeps that love vibrant and alive.

Mickey: I could see that.

Me: So, it's kind of tricky. I have to make myself known to them—but not *so* known that they lose the free will to consciously choose me.

Mickey: Wow. Pretty complicated!

Me: Certain aspects of it really are. Physically, their system will at least appear almost exquisitely simple —

which in some ways it is, since it's based on the idea that mathematical truths expressed in form tend to....

Mickey: Whoa, your Lordship.

Me: What?

Mickey: Math? I think you know how I — how we all — feel about math, Lord.

Me: You know, a lot of cherubim and seraphim happen to *like* math, Mickey.

Mickey: Shall I send one of them in, Lord? I'm sure I can find one if you just give me a few eons....

Me: Oh, Mickey. You're just so darn...what's the word I'm looking for...replaceable?

Mickey: And you're so...what's the word I'm looking for...?

Me: Not?

Mickey: No, that's not it....

_Me:_ Ha! You kill me! For the life of me, Mickey, I simply cannot understand how it can be that I'm God, but _you're_ the funny one.

Mickey: Just another of your unfathomable miracles, Your Majesty.

_Me:_ Thank Me you use it for good, instead of for evil.

Mickey: "Evil," my Lord?

_Me:_ Yes, Mickey. Evil.

Mickey: What's the matter? What's that look on your face? I've never seen you look like that before. You're scaring me, Lord.

_Me:_ Oh, I'm sorry, Mickey. It's just . . . the whole evil thing.

Mickey: What is "evil," Lord?

_Me:_ Oh, it's nothing you need to worry about, my little friend. And it's _definitely_ not anything you need to know about.

Mickey: Well, whatever it is, it's surely nothing you can't handle, right, Lord?

Me: That's right, Mickey. I'll take care of it.

Mickey: It's impossible to doubt you.

Me: But, Mickey, I want you to promise me something. I want you to promise me that you will never get curious about evil. That you will never try to discover what it is, or how it works, or why it works, or anything about it. Promise me that you won't.

Mickey: Of course I promise, Father. Why would I want to get involved with anything you're so obviously against? What would make *anyone* want to do such a thing? What is it? What did I say? Why are you laughing, Lord? I don't think I've ever seen you laugh so hard! You are laughing, right, Lord? Lord? Are you laughing? Or are you crying?

But Wait! There's More

Okay—so, that was really fun. It reminded me of the days I used to work with Shakespeare.

Um—_not!_

Anyway, you know what? Now I feel like writing an entire book. Nothing as huge as my _first_ one, of course — but...something.

So. What to write, what to write...?

Oh, I know. I want to write something addressing how often nowadays Christianity is considered as little if anything more than a repressive, fear-based, guilt-driven, woman-hating, sin-obsessed, money-hungry, homophobic monolith of an institution led by sanctimonious, hypocritical windbags shrilly braying about who and what I do and don't approve of, and what I intend to do about it.

Seriously: That nonsense drives me insane. And it also drives legions upon legions of good, thoughtful, strong, loving, _sane_ people as far away from me as they can possibly get.

Man. Talk about wrong.

So I think I'll take the time, right now, to set the record straight about who I really am, what I really think, and why I do the things that I do.

John here won't mind. (*It's true! I won't!*)

And, let's face it: It's not like we're taking a vote here. Hah!

It *is* good to be king!

BEING OBJECTIONABLE

So what I'll do is present below the reasons/questions/ objections that (I happen to know) nonbelievers are most likely to cite if asked, say, why exactly it is that they'd rather have a thistle jammed up one of their nostrils than to even consider becoming Christian.

Then I'll answer those objections.

Ah, the Q & A approach. What a classic!

And now what I need is a source for those complaints; I need to zip out there, and get into the minds of people who believe they don't like me, and find out why they feel that way.

Cuz it's all about keeping it real, man. No solipsism for *me*.

So. Be right back.

And I'm back. I went out, did a...um...*scan* on a Statistically Representative selection of Firm Atheists, and isolated how they would and do articulate their specific problems with the idea of my Actual Viability.

Man. Such *walls* some people have.

It's really quite the bummer.

Anyway, what I'll do is present here the most *trenchant* of the complaints against me that I located within non believers out there—and then follow each of those pithy proclamations or quarrelsome queries with my direct response to it.

Perfect! Can't beat it with a stick. I'll (again—and so to speak) nail down some of this stuff, John here will have a surprisingly productive morning, and before too long non-believers-in-me everywhere will be able to have the weird experience of wondering whether or not theirs was the brain from which I pulled one or all of the following objections to me.

How fun!

Listen: If you who are now reading this go on to find that I/we failed to touch upon your primary concern with the faith, or if you would like a more detailed, personal response to any of the questions below, please pray to me about it, and I'll be sure to get right back to you. (Actually, that really *is* a much more effective way for us to communicate. But this works, too.)

Okay, then! Let's check out the Big Beefs with Me, shall we?

I just don't believe in God, period.

Well, I guess all I can say to that Blunt Affront is: Ffpttrr ploooziipert veempi, coippop fip greetnk. Feekgreegputnup lirsceek nerschnit. Plerrfup!

Get it? Cuz you aren't gonna understand me anyway?

One thing is certain: There's no way you don't believe in me because I'm not funny. Not possible. I mean, you've read at least *some* of the Bible, haven't you? Talk about funny! Did you read the part where . . . ? Or that other part, where . . . ?

Well, for a lot of that stuff you really had to be there.

But what about penguins? You've seen those, haven't you? I mean, c'mon! They're upright bird-fish *with no legs!* Just huge floppy feet! Automatically funny! And have you considered the dung beetle? Hello? *Dung beetle?* The thing's whole *life* is pushing around giant dung balls!

And you think there's no God.

What is the *matter* with you?

No, but seriously: I really am deeply grieved that you and I don't exactly see eye-to-eye on the whole question of my existence. And what you're not believing in me really and truly _does_ make me want to say to you is, "Good luck"—and mean it with all my heart, too. Because you, my friend, have an extremely difficult row to hoe. Because not believing in a God means that you're stuck being as alone in this world as anyone can be—or at least feeling that you are, which amounts to the same thing. _Nobody_ is lonelier than an atheist. Sure, you have friends and loved ones, and while they can certainly go a long way toward bringing you that sense of enduring peace humans naturally crave, they can't go anywhere near all the way. And not believing in any sort of Omnipotent Co-Participant means that when those people aren't around you, you are _seriously_ alone. And that just makes for a lot of really hard moments in life—or, worse in a way, for a very long, slow grind.

What's particularly difficult about living a life without any sort of conscious awareness of Me is that it means you're necessarily left to battle your demons all by yourself. And by "demons," _please_ understand that

41

I mean nothing more (though nothing less!) than that very real force that . . . well, for one, that keeps you doing things that you know are, at the very least, not especially wonderful for you. And that probably aren't exactly lighting up the lives of those around you, either.

Saying that you can't stop doing "bad" or troubling things is *not* any sort of value judgment. It has nothing to do with religion, or any kind of moral calculation, or anything like that. It has to do with being human — period. Being human means that, no matter who you are or what you do or don't believe in, you really, *really* wish you could quit doing things like:

- Being such an aggressive, short-tempered pain in the patoot
- Being so lazy
- Eating like a dumpster
- Drinking like you can always buy a new liver at Wal-Mart (You can't yet, can you?)
- Smoking
- Catching fire in the first place

- Not laughing at God's jokes
- Watching so much TV
- Getting high
- Worrying about money so much
- Worrying about anything so much
- Being addicted to pornography
- Failing professionally
- Choosing isolation over companionship
- Having no idea what you're doing with your life
- Feeling like such a loser all the time

You almost desperately want to quit doing these sorts of things _because you're human_. _All_ humans want to better themselves; you _all_ struggle to overcome those behaviors or thoughts that you know work against your better interests. If you can deny that that struggle plays a, if not _the_, major role in your life, then you are either lying, very young (and so haven't yet had the time to experience the hard, rough walls of who you are closing in around you), or you're ignoring a tremendous amount of information about yourself and the way you live.

Either way, it's inevitable that one day you're going to need help. Real help. And not the kind your friends or family can give you, either. Because as close as some people are to you, *none* of them are so close they can reach down inside your soul and instantly restructure the very core of your identity.

Because that would be my job.

It's simple: Just like every other person in the history of the world, you need help making yourself happier. People who believe in God turn to God for help with that struggle. That's what people *do.* That's what God is *for.*

Um ... not that I'm trying to bully or scare you into believing in me or anything. I'm just saying that sooner or later (and, lucky you, it'll probably be later — assuming you don't get hit by a bus tomorrow, or, Me forbid, struck by lightning or anything), you're extremely likely to rethink the whole "Who Needs God?" thing.

And that moment, despite the agony it will cause you to reach it, is one to which I cannot help but look forward.

There are two times atheists suddenly start praying to me: When things are promising to physically snuff the life out of them or someone they love, and when they finally realize that they are, in very real terms, absolutely powerless to stop something inside of themselves that has or is about to destroy their lives.

The former is obviously a more dramatic, immediate sort of thing. I make a lot of new best friends in fires and earthquakes and war and so on.

The latter is a more personal, private thing. I get a lot of alcoholics, drug addicts, and prisoners that way.

The rest usually contact me on their deathbed — when, all at once, the Mother of All Bill Collectors comes a-knockin'.

Not a good moment if you haven't spent your life exactly balancing your accounts.

You know that smell you always smell in an old folks' home? A lot of that is deep and sudden _fear._

When reality wins, atheists lose. And atheists _always_ lose, because if you don't believe that some superseding, benevolent presence is overseeing the universe and your life in it, then inevitably your natural optimism and hope run out of gas. And a person without hope is, or always becomes, more animal than human.

So here is what I would like to suggest, my atheistic friend. (And I mean that: Who am I to find fault with someone who has done nothing more "wrong" than to believe in the power of the free will I so painstakingly gave and maintain?) Would you please consider taking me for a test ride? After all, you believe in the power of ideas. You're a genuine free thinker. Your whole *thing* is to be unafraid of the mind, to believe in its integrity and flexibility. (And, again: Bravo!)

So, then, it wouldn't, like, kill you or anything, would it, to spend three days — only three days! — pretending that I exist?

It wouldn't!

Besides, ninety-five percent of all people in the history of the world believe in a God. Ninety-five percent! (I'm sure that statistic is correct, by the way, because I found it on the Internet.) Well, you love people, right? You trust in the inherent, ultimate value of the human experience. So it's natural that you should want to share something of the experience that is so central to the lives of so many people, right?

So for three days, do. Join the flock, Lambchops. Pretend to believe in me.

The only thing I ask is that you really do try to take it seriously. You have to imagine that you really _do_ believe I'm up here. And that I love you. And that loving you is actually the entire purpose of my existence—that it's the only thing I've ever done, or cared to do.

For three days walk around, and live your life, and all the while imagine that everything you see, and everything that happens to you, is a gift from me to you—that it's there because I am using it to try to tell you something. As often as you can remember to, imagine that I'm embracing you, smiling over you, loving you. Imagine that I'm delighted with you. (Because I am! I am! I am!) Imagine that my love for you is so great that it lifts away from you, forever and ever, whatever guilt you feel for whatever things you've done.

Imagine that cleansing you that way is possible for me because I am God. And imagine that I know how it feels to _be_ cleansed that way because I've been human.

Imagine that that little internal voice that's been with you all of your life — the one telling you that you're important, and special, and absolutely perfect *exactly* the way you are — has been me, all along.

You do that. For three days, you test-drive me like that. And then we'll see where we're at on day four.

If you really exist, why don't you prove it?

Wouldn't it be funny if the moment you asked that question you dropped dead?

No, you're right. That wouldn't be funny at all. Sorry. Bad God.

Here's the Real Deal about that question: Its answer lies in the question itself.

Hey! Just like Yoda!

Me, I loved that guy. After that movie came out, I spent about a month up here looking exactly like him. I had the ears, the little walking stick, everything. Freaked out my angels like you wouldn't believe.

"Don't play the harp," I would say. "Let the harp play you."

Ah. Good times.

Anyway, the answer to that question really *does* lie in the question. It *is* the question. In other words, if I were to suddenly present irrefutable proof of my existence, all humans would immediately lose the capacity to ask that or any other question.

You see why, right? Like, let's say one day you're walking along, when suddenly the vast blue sky above you is rent open, and there, taking up most of what used to be the sky, you (along with everybody else in the world) behold my Massive Visage, looking down upon the earth.

"Hello, people of Earth!" I say. "It is I, your God and Father, Holiest of Holies, Most High on High, Very God of Very God, creator and sustaining force of All That Is. I hear a lot of you are wondering whether or not I exist. The first time I came down there is not, I suppose, doing it for you anymore. So behold: I exist already! I'm here! I'm real! Worship me! Love me! Let me love you! And let's clean up those oceans, shall we? I now return you to your regularly programmed sky. See you at church!"

Now, that'd be great, right? Because you and everyone else in the world would finally have certain knowledge of my existence. *Except everybody's free will would be gone! Poof! Gone! Just like that!*

The creatures that I now so love and adore would instantly transmogrify into a race of Brain-Dead Belief Zombies.

And none of us want that. But that would have happened the second I went Teletubby Sun on you, because from that moment on you wouldn't have any choice in the world *but* to believe in me. I would have snatched that choice right away from you.

The good news, for me, is that you'd finally come to me; the bad news — for both of us — is that you'd arrive missing the very quality that now makes you you: Your mind. Your will. Your Me-given right to choose.

Everything you are lies in the fact that you are absolutely free to believe whatever you care to. You can believe, for instance, that it's a purely mechanistic universe, and that you and all your fellow humanoids descended from chimpanzees. (A theory, you should know, that I find entirely plausible. I'm down for it having gone: water; amoeba in water; bigger amoeba in water; big amoeba with gills in water; fish in water; fish flopping about on land; fish crawling about on land; landlubber fish sprouting fur; furry, landlubber fish resentful of fins when trying to climb trees; monkeys in trees; monkeys on ground; monkeys with sharp sticks; monkeys with lots of food and dead enemies everywhere; humans. Works

51

for me!) If you'd rather not be a monkey's uncle, you can believe people descended from crawdads. You can believe giant crawdads from outer space landed on earth eight million years ago and mutated into humans when giant meteors shot past earth and sprayed them all with radioactive gamma-gamma waves.

You can think that makes perfect sense on Tuesday, and on Wednesday maintain that that's absolutely ridiculous — that they were beta-beta waves.

And while you're honing your theory of evolution, you're free to enjoy a nice, delicious glass of Coca-Cola. Or Pepsi. Or Dr. Dew, or whatever it's called. Or a cup of green tea. Or dandelion tea. Or crabgrass tea. Or something else that doesn't taste like dirt.

And while you're enjoying your refreshing beverage at, say, an outdoor café, and thinking about giant mutating crawdads from outer space, you can pause in your rumination long enough to say a kind word to a passerby. You can be nice to your waiter. Or you can be obnoxious to your waiter: You can steal his tip off another table and then run away without paying for your dandelion tea. You can pull out a gun and start *shooting* at your waiter if you want to.

Because you are free to do any Me-damned thing you want to!

Because that is how I made you.

What am I, stupid? Love is my nature. It's what I *am.* "Jesus is Love" is by far my favorite bumper-sticker. (Although "The Lord is Coming — Look Busy" rates a very close second.) My primary purpose in creating human beings was so that they would love me as much as I love them. Love *needs* expression and reciprocation. I didn't have anyone to love — much less to love me back.

So I created people!

I created you!

You little love-dove, you.

But it wouldn't work if I made it so you *had* to love me. Nobody wants to force, or trick, anyone into loving them. That's not love. That's…politics. Or show business. Or public relations. Or some other thing people should really stop doing.

The point is that if I provided you with irrefutable proof that I exist, you'd suddenly become someone whose allegiance to me really wouldn't mean all that much, either to you or me.

Another humongous reason I don't (again) objectively prove my existence to great numbers of people at once is because my Entire Purpose is to have a deep and exquisitely intimate relationship with each and every *individual.* There's just no applicable, practical context for doing the Mass Presentation thing. It's not my will to exist *outside* of your life. My proper relationship to you is as *part* of you: part of your soul, your psychological matrix, your whole...*life.* Manifesting myself into your physical reality is just so...not that. It wouldn't work. Coming to you from the outside can only negate the possibility of our developing the only relationship that could possibly do you any good. And that relationship is me, inside you.

Oh, behaaave, you cheeky monkey.

Ha! Another great movie!

Yeah, baby, *yeah!* (I don't even want to tell you what happened up here when I started walking around like Austin Powers. Let's just say it's best when a choir of heavenly angels _doesn't_ try to work the word "shagali-cious" into a celestial hymn.)

Anyway, you see (I hope) what I mean about how it just wouldn't work if I ever _really_ proved myself to you. Like, let's say one Thursday night you're at home watching TV or something — or, better, that you're sitting on your couch, thinking, "I have _so_ already seen this episode of _Friends_. And cable has yet again managed to somehow have nothing but brain-numbing crap on any of its six hundred channels. Man, I wish I had positive proof there's a God, so that my life could have a little meaning" — and _bam_ I appear, radiant with the non-blinding glory of a thousand suns, right there between your entertainment center and your plastic ficus tree.

"Hi, there," I say. "I'm God. I really exist. Nice place you have here."

Take it from me: You would instantly fall to your knees and begin crying and confessing your sins. Your hysterical regret and shameless fear would be terrible to behold. Every wrong you ever did, every lie you ever told, every time you ever chose to elevate yourself by hurting another would come roaring back to you, burning into your soul like the fires of hell that at that moment would seem so real to you you'd wish you were wearing asbestos underpants.

About a half hour later, your tears would have largely abated, and, confession-wise, you'd be down to telling me that you secretly covet your neighbor's SUV and don't floss as often as you know you should. It wouldn't be long after that before your knees would be aching so much you'd struggle back up to your feet to relieve them. Then — because you're a good person who likes to share good things with others — you'd ask me whether or not I'd mind if you phoned a few of your friends to let them know you've got God in your living room. And I, being a reasonable sort of omnipotent being, would say sure, go ahead.

"I'm not kidding!" you'd cry into the phone. "It's *God!* Right by my entertainment center! He's not as tall as you'd think! Bring sunglasses! Hurry!"

And then your friends would all rush over to your place — and they, too, would be amazed. And they too would drop to their knees, crying and confessing their sins, and verily your apartment would be filled with the sounds of wailing and gnashing of teeth.

But before long your friends, too, would be all confessed out—and their knees would be killing them also. So up they'd come.

Pretty soon they'd all be wandering around your apartment, looking for tissues or for something to eat or drink, because, after all, one can really work up an appetite wailing and gnashing one's teeth.

And I'd still be hanging out over there by the entertainment center. Checking out your CD collection. Noticing your ficus needs dusting. Enjoying a cracker, maybe.

After a while one of your friends would say something like, "Wow! God! I can't believe I met God! My parents will _die_ when they hear this! It's unbelievable! I'm _definitely_ going to start going to church now. I really am. Wow! You really exist! Boy, that's just amazing. Just...amazing. Whew. Boy. Well, listen, I've got this stupid meeting at work first thing tomorrow morning, so I guess I better get going. But thanks again for inviting me over to see God. I _definitely_ owe you dinner or something. It's been _great!_ Gimme a call tomorrow night, okay? And you, God.

What can I say? You really *are* awesome. Keep up the good work, okay? Seriously, you're doing great, no matter what anyone says. And that stuff back there, where I was crying about needing a new car? It's not really that big a deal, okay? I mean, sure it'd be *great* — and I'm definitely down for that Mercedes I was mentioning — but I'm sure I can get a few more miles out of my Camry. I just need a good mechanic, that's all. And, hey, if you have any recommendations in that regard, that'd be good enough for me! Anyway, thanks again for everything. I guess I'll see you in church! Bye, everybody!"

And before long everyone else would be filing out of your place.

And then it would just be you and I, again.

And by then it would be too late to watch Letterman.

So we'd microwave some popcorn, and see who was on Conan.

The point is, I can only be real to one person at a time — and I operate from the inside out, not from the outside in. It just can't work any other way. I hope I've been clear about why.

What's the deal with evil, anyway? Why does a God who is all-powerful and all-compassionate allow evil to exist? He either wills evil to exist—which makes him despicable—or he's powerless to stop it, which makes him uninspiringly weak, to say the least. Both bite. What's up?

Did you know that "evil," spelled backward, is "live"?

Sideways, it's "veil."

Inside-out, it's "vile."

Which I think just about says it all, don't you?

(I'm kidding, of course. But isn't it weird how it really kind of *does?*)

This question is the One Big Toughie. It's the argument that throughout history has been most often used to refute Christianity. If evil is real, it goes, then Christianity can't be.

Fine. Drop the Biggie Bomb right in the middle of my book. Wonderful. But let me ask you something: Do I come over to your place and ask you how in the world you can imagine yourself a person of taste, and still have that *couch?* Do I? No. Have I ever looked through your medicine cabinet and then exclaimed, "Boy, for a person who claims to have his act together, you sure do have a lot of *ointments* in there."

No. Because that would be wrong.

Actually, this brings me to a good starting point for this conversation, which is that I *might* come over to your house and make fun of your couch or the contents of your medicine cabinet. I mean, I wouldn't, because I'm God and prefer not to make Rude House Calls. But I *could* — and that's the point.

Just like you're free to do whatever you want — be it as rude, mean, or even cruel as you'd like.

Perhaps you see where I'm going with this.

It's a simple fact of the human experience that people do horrible things all the time. And so when people ask me why evil exists in the world, what they are (usually) asking is why I allow people to act in monstrous ways.

Within recent human history, for instance, was the terrible tragedy now called "9/11." Thousands of innocent people, wiped out. An unthinkable horror. And one that caused a lot of people to wonder where *I* was when it happened—and why I didn't stop it.

I'll tell you where I was when those planes hit those buildings. I was the same place I am whenever anyone is victimized by anyone else: in sheer, mortal agony.

Imagine how you would feel if you saw one of your children violently murdering one of your other children. Same thing—only three thousand times over. Except that you could maybe *stop* children from murdering one another. In a very real sense, I cannot stop anyone from visiting terror upon anyone else. I mean, of course I *could* stop any individual act of evil—I'm God. I could stop all of them, instantly. But the truth is (and I hesitate to even say this, for fear that it might in any way at all sound as if I don't utterly identify with any and every person who has ever suffered), you wouldn't truly want me to do that.

Again: It's *all* about human free will.

Over and over and over and over again: *Everything* in your world and in your consciousness—evil included—is predicated upon the fact that you and everyone else in the world can feel, think, and do whatever you want.

If I made it so that the only way people could do what they wanted was if they wanted to do something *good,* then two things would happen. First, people, having in very short order realized that they have pretty much zero control over their lives, would lapse into Numbed Apathy faster than you can say, "Gee, what a surprise: fat-free ice cream again." Second, the very meaning of "good" would be eradicated — what with there being nothing to compare it to, and all.

So. We'd have a planet full of people bored into a stupor who have no context for understanding relative morality.

If that doesn't say "Paaaaaarty!" then I didn't invent sea anemones.

The terribly frightful and fundamental fact about human free will is that, as a condition of its existence, people are free to do all the evil they can stomach. And this means that if I'm going to eliminate evil, I'm going to have to snatch your free will away from you so fast you'd never even know you had it.

You wouldn't know there ever *was* anything but fat-free ice cream.

Think about it.

Freedom of Choice vs. No Evil.

I mean, you've had Ben and Jerry's "Cherry Garcia" ice cream, right?

Man. Talk about sinfully delicious.

Um. I mean... I've heard it's great.

Try to imagine a life where choosing to enjoy a delicious ice cream, or to... I don't know... get the Sunday paper delivered to your house, isn't even an option.

Worse: Try to imagine that the only flavor ice cream came in was garlic. Or fried hamster. Or Chunky Puke. Or that the only publication you could ever get delivered to your house was Grain Silo Monthly, or Ham Radio Today, or something. (No offense to farmers and ham radio enthusiasts, of course. I personally would _love_ either of those publications.)

Now imagine you didn't care, because you didn't know the difference.

Now imagine if you couldn't even imagine imagining that.

See? Without choices, you wouldn't even be human; you'd be a lobotomized automaton from the planet Vapid.

And I pray it's clear that we really are talking about an All or None proposition here. In order to rid the world of evil, I can't *sometimes* take away people's free will. I can't stop it in some instances, and allow it in others. For one, there's no way to categorically determine at what point a thing becomes evil. In other words, I couldn't stop murder without stopping thoughts of murder. And I couldn't stop thoughts of murder without stopping thoughts of any sort of physical retribution. Which would mean stopping anyone from thinking angry thoughts.

Which would mean, of course, the end of all freeway driving.

You see my point: I've either got to let people be completely free, or I've got to essentially follow them around with a ruler to rap them on the knuckles with whenever they do or think anything that's even *close* to being wrong.

That said, though, you can rest assured that I do get as involved in trying to mitigate acts of evil as I can without in any way making my presence conclusively apparent. I know that may seem hard to believe, given the scope and scale of so much human tragedy. But it's true. It's why things could have _always_ been worse (though, again, I realize how often that sounds unacceptably callous). It's a bizarre thing to hear God say, I know, but the fact is that I do what I can. I scream at people's consciousness when I'm trying to stop them from doing harm. People can be really dedicated to doing evil, though. Agonizingly, I constantly have to simply let go, and watch what happens.

It is, though, important to remember and trust in the fact that I _do_ take care of evil's victims. Either their suffering, in real time, ceases — which tends to leave people more sensitive to the pain of others, and much more likely to believe in me, both of which are beautiful things — or their suffering brings an end to their corporal existence, in which case they are ushered into my presence.

That said, it is my hope that you can see that evil does not exist because I'm incapable of stopping it, nor because I "allow" it to. Evil exists because I allow _you_ to exist.

Lose humans; lose evil.
Keep humans; keep evil.
Talk about your Catch-22, 'eh?

◆ ◆ ◆

Now, besides human evil, there is, of course, all that evil that *isn't* generated by humans: death and decay, say, or hurricanes and earthquakes and so on. What we might call natural evil. You may be wondering why I "allow" all that stuff to exist: Why I would allow cancer or AIDS, for instance.

Well, here's the deal with that: I hate cancer, okay? I hate AIDS. I hate fever blisters. I hate *anything* that hurts or harms people. A little kid in Peru gets a splinter in his finger, and I'm rolling around on the clouds, cursing the day I ever dreamed up wood.

I'm reminded of that American politician — that recent one, that guy from Arkansas — who used to always say, "I feel your pain." If I went into politics, I'd be like *that* guy.

Whoa — hold on a sec. Let me go check my records.

Okay, I wouldn't be *exactly* like that guy.

Yowzer. Talk about blowing a wonderful opportunity to...well, let's just stop right there, shall we?

The point is: Everything that hurts you hurts me. _Everything._

◆ ◆ ◆

Now I want to tell you something that I think might sound a little...well, I have no idea how it might sound. Obnoxiously self-serving, probably. But here's a truth: You would not _believe_ how much of what is now considered an "act of God" could be prevented or radically mitigated if everyone down there on Ol' Blue Skies would pool their resources and start working together, instead of spending so much time and energy working against one another.

The human race has _so_ much more power than it realizes. You're all about one discovery away — from something like, say, how sound waves can be compressed and harnessed to interact with matter—from practically putting me out of a job.

I'm serious. If everyone on earth, right now, began truly adhering to the "One for All, and All for One!" creed, in about twenty years you'd be living in a world so different from the one you're in right now you'd think you were on another planet.

Which, come to think of it, you could actually be.

In other words, no fair complaining about what you can't do before you've done everything you can. No fair throwing up your hands, when rolling up your sleeves is all that's needed. If you can't grasp something, maybe it just means you haven't opened up your arms wide enough.

A bird in the hand is worth two in the bush.

A stitch in time saves nine.

A penny saved is like a dime earned after taxes.

A babbling God is better than no God at all.

What I'm saying is this: There was a little boy in Ethiopia who would have cured cancer, if only he hadn't died of starvation.

Why are so many Christians so obnoxious and mean-spirited?
It seems like Christianity's mostly about being judgmental, narrow-minded, and having an infuriatingly condescending attitude toward anyone who *isn't* a Christian. Christians are so busy being smug about being Christian that they forget to be *kind*.

Oh, come on, now—don't you think that's a little harsh?

After all, remember: Christians aren't perfect; they're just forgiven.

So they're only imperfect for, like, brief moments at a time.

And then they're better than you again.

No, but seriously, if the above statement reflects your own sentiments, then when you die I am going to snatch you right up into heaven and give you a seat right next to mine. Because verily I say unto you: You have been doinked.

It pains me beyond anything I could possibly express to say that I understand how you came by your impression of Christianity. That you feel this way is a shame, in the most profound sense of that word. All the Christians you've ever spent any time with at all should have deeply impressed you with their great, fun character. That that didn't happen is as wrong as wrong gets.

You may also, I know, feel negatively toward Christianity because you're aware of the ways throughout history that Christians have behaved abominably.

But, for now, let's say that your agreement with the opening statement has less to do with your dissatisfaction with Christianity's history than it does with your dissatisfaction with a lot of the Christians you've met. Even if you knew that five hundred years ago, in my name, the Spanish Inquisition committed unthinkable atrocities to an unthinkable number of people, or that three hundred years ago Christian missionaries responded to the love and open arms of the people welcoming them to the New World by starving and beating them into submission, if the only Christians you'd ever met were deeply ashamed of the less-then-peachy aspects of their faith's history and were themselves open, thoughtful, admirable people, you'd feel better about Christianity in general, right?

Right.

But, instead, you've met the dreaded, despicable Bad Christians.

Man. Just thinking about the BCs gives me the fantods.

Please allow me, right off the bat, to grant you this: Christians (or at least people who think or say they're Christians) are just about the only people in the world who will screw you till you bleed, and then tell you it was for your own good. Most people just hammer you and go on their way: You're an incidental victim in the vast minefield of their obnoxiousness. But Christians will tell you they slammed you to the ground like a flaming bag of swamp peat so that you could learn something about being more pleasing to me, or to help rid you of sin, or some other nonsense that makes me want to reach out of the sky and clamp those offensive prigs and just *hold* them there while they rethink the purpose of their life.

Man, that stuff drives me crazy.

Trust me: If I want to teach you something, I will. Nothing in this universe angers me like someone doing anyone any kind of harm in my name. *Any* kind of harm. I hate it more than anything I know.

I mean, imagine how Walt Disney would feel if bands of marauding Mickeys were going around mugging and beating people, while saying, "Walt wants you to suffer! Walt wants you to die! We're breaking your legs cuz that's what *Walt* wants!"

You'd be lying on the ground going, "I hate Walt Disney. Help!"

See? Not good for Walt; not good for you; not good for Disneyland.

On the other hand, though, we do have to be fair. You feel the way you do about Christians because of the Christians you've met, right? But, being Reasonable Types, you are obliged to acknowledge that in your life you've also met a bunch of really good people who are Christian: kind, thoughtful, patient, strong, funny, smart, *normal* people. There's just no way for you to have met a lot of offensive Christians without having also met at least an equal number of people who clearly and consistently rocketh.

(Um...this is assuming that you live in a place where you've necessarily met or known a wide range of people who think of themselves as Christian. But of course I understand how it might be that if you live in, say, a remote little village in a distinctly non-Christian country, and the only Christians you've ever met are missionaries who've apparently vowed not to rest until every last one of the "natives" in the area signs a statement declaring their own genitals to be Public Enemy No. 1, then you might be something less than thrilled about the whole "Let's Be Christians" thing. I understand that — and, again, please allow me to apologize for those people. If you really _have_ only ever met Bad Christians, then, as I say, I'll be sure to save you a seat.)

But if you live around many Christians, then you must agree that you've known or heard about some good ones, just as you've known (or heard about) some bad. It's true enough that you can barely throw a rock without hitting some kind of soup kitchen, hospital, senior housing project, or Rescue Mission founded or being run by Christians.

Here's the thing: It's the Dreaded BCs who get all the attention. Everyone looks at the guy who starts screaming at the bus stop. Nobody pays any attention to the person who's just quietly sitting there, waiting for a bus (and maybe praying for the screaming psycho). Real Christians, people who genuinely Get It, are grounded, sane human beings who take care of their business — who love their family, love me, and try their best to leave the world a better place than they found it. They're not on TV, raving about the sins of this or the sins of that. They're not trying to finagle little old ladies into sending them all their money. They're not standing on a street corner screaming at passersby about how they're going to hell. Of course you see *those* guys. Everybody sees *those* guys. *I* sure see them — and they make me cringe, every time.

And what the more, shall we say, attention-generating Christians sometimes miss, is that they have absolutely no more access to me than your brain and heart afford you. I don't care how large a following someone has, or how gargantuan a person's church, ranch, or hair is:

There's no Boss Of The Christians. (Um ... except me. And, sorry to say, business is down — so you're fired. Sorry! As a severance package, we're going to let you keep your company calendar. Ha! Just kidding! Now get back to work.)

The point is that there are hypocritical, judgmental creepazoids everywhere, in every kind of group or class you can think of. You get more than three people together, and it's a safe bet you'll barely be able to stand two of them. That's just life. So, yeah, some Christians need to be taken out into a field and pushed into a ditch — but so what? That doesn't mean Christianity is bad, any more than a broken pencil means writing or drawing is bad. They're simply unrelated.

Some people are immature. Some aren't. If you found a pebble in a bag of beans, you wouldn't assume all the beans are rocks. You'd throw the rock out — and get on preparing the beans. (Mmmm ... beans.) No problem.

Plus, always remember: Ultimate Justice is a _huge_ part of what I do. In other words, rest assured that as surely as meanies get fewer cards on Valentine's Day, I will take care of the Offensive Ones. _Life_ will take care of them.

That's an inherent characteristic of the system in which you live. The strident "Christians," for instance, who offend you with that weak Holier Than Thou nonsense, are in pain. They're not happy, they're not balanced, things don't go their way. Nobody sends them valentines.

The truth (as you know) is that you should feel sorry for the people who seem like they could give a hang whether you feel sorry for them or not. Because as awful as it is being around an obnoxious, nasty person, it's infinitely better than *being* an obnoxious, nasty person.

It's the wounded animals who bite the hardest.

Anyway, the Bad Christians will be all right. They'll get it. If they keep praying, meditating, going to church, and hanging out with good Christians, they'll smooth out.

You don't have to worry about them, in other words. Your heart, right now, tells you what is right. If people who claim to be Christians rub you the wrong way, ignore them — and assume they rub me the wrong way, too. (You can also assume that I have a broader view of them than you do. I know all kinds of things about them you couldn't possibly. You see the effect of their pain; I see its cause. So I'll naturally have a slightly more compassionate view of them than you're likely to. But still! No excuses for them!)

Listen, the entire point of Christianity is that people are supposed to love each other. That's its purpose. The whole Christian Program goes like this: I came down; I absorbed into my body all the guilt that anyone could ever cause or feel (since guilt is _the_ thing that interferes with love, and so Must Go); as a symbol of my For All Time eradication of that guilt I let be killed the body that held it; the entire time I was down there I made it as clear as I possibly could that the whole reason for my coming and doing that was so that people would actually believe it had really and truly happened; believing in the reality of my sacrifice establishes the means by which any person, anywhere in the world, at any time in their life, can, by appealing to me and my experience on the cross, have lifted from them any amount of guilt, so that once again they'll be free to love themselves as, Me knows, I do, and can then go back out into the world, filled with nothing but love, love, _love_.

The End.

That's it. That's The Plan. Most get it; some don't; some do on Thursday, but then forget it on Saturday.

Let's make a deal: You don't judge Christianity by the weenie Christians you know, and I won't judge your whole life by those few and far between times when you aren't exactly at your best, either.

See? We'll look past the negative. We'll believe in something better. We'll *forgive*.

What's that whole "Atonement" thing actually *mean?*

The At One-ment (Hey! I'm Hooked on Phonics!™ Wait—no I'm not) refers to that act in which I allowed myself to get brutally murdered so that all humans could be forever cleansed of the guilt associated with the things they do or think that do not, shall we say, represent their finest moments.

I let myself be tortured to death so that you could live free of pain.

But, hey, no *pressure* or anything. I don't want you worrying about it. I was glad to do it. Seriously. No problem. It was a Friday. I really didn't have all that much to do but hang around anyway.

For three days.

I was just killing time.

Oh, don't I just slay you?

Cuz I sure do me.

Speaking of which, why don't we revisit the final moment of my human life as recorded in the Bible? Here's the last of that experience, as remembered by that prophet to end all prophets, the inimitable John:

Later, knowing that all was now completed, and so that the Scripture would be fulfilled, Jesus said, "I am thirsty." A jar of wine vinegar was there, so they soaked a sponge in it, put the sponge on a stalk of the hyssop plant, and lifted it to Jesus' lips. When he had received the drink, Jesus said, "It is finished." With that, he bowed his head and gave up his spirit.

So. There's that.

You know, when you're dying from a prolonged beating while nailed to a giant wooden cross by iron spikes hammered through your hands and feet, nothing says "refreshing" like a filthy sponge full of wine vinegar being smeared all over your face.

And it leaves you feeling so dignified, too.

Ahh. *Not* good times.

Still, there was a job to do, and I was the man to do it. And so I did: The "it" in "It is finished" refers to the establishment of the means by which all people, forever, could have access to real and lasting salvation. I know

I just said this, but if anything in the universe bears repeating, it's that what my dying on the cross secured was the means by which, from that point on, all human beings could have rinsed from their hearts and minds their guilt (however "naturally" they acquired it), which, without my divine intervention, must otherwise fester inside of them, where at best it severely undermines the quality of their lives and at worst compels them to contribute to that wretched, twisted cause that seeks to drag all of humankind down into the pits of degradation.

Do you see? I won the battle between good and evil by paying, in full, with my body, any and all karmic debt that might ever be incurred by anyone doing evil.

You might owe the phone company, the electric company, the credit card company, and your landlord. But you don't owe _me_, or the world, anything. I've already totaled you out.

I've already _atoned_ for your sins.

Which means that you and I, forever, are copasetic.

As long as you believe in me, that is. As long as you believe that as the Christ I took human form and stepped into human history for the specific purpose of removing from all people — by which I most definitely and forever mean from *you personally* — the debt incurred by any and all sin.

Believe that, and it's all about you and me, friend.

Don't, and you're on your own.

But you believe it. You have to. Cuz you know who's on your side, don't you? You know who's got you covered, don't you? You're feeling the love. You know you are. C'mon. Admit it. Who loves you? Who? Who cares about you? Who gave his all so you could delight in life instead of being bogged down by true existential angst?

Who's your daddy?

That's right: Me. The Father. Jesus. The Holy Ghost.

Us.

I.

And what do really good fathers do? That's right: They fork over the big bucks to cover the cost of every single thing their kids could ever think of doing.

Do you really wonder why such infinite numbers of people have always signed on for Team Jesus? Do you *really* think they're all just lazy, shallow simpletons?

Well, they're not. What they *are* is debt-free. Which is to say that, spiritually speaking, they're forgiven.

Forgiven!

By God Almighty!

Forever!

Man, I just don't know what else you could possibly want from me.

Isn't it enough that I believe in God? Why do I have to narrow it down to the *Christian* God?

Well, let's take those two questions one at a time, if that's cool. (It is? Great!)

No. And because it's the best one.

That was easy. *Next!*

Okay, can we at least agree that I'm the *funniest* of your Big God options? Can we? Because I really don't see how that's debatable. When's the last time you got a decent yuk out of any of your *other* deity options?

Never, that's when.

Don't forget, it isn't just that penguins spend their whole lives without knees. They don't have *necks*, either! Amazing! They're nothing but giant flapper feet, torsos, and *beaks*!

Man. All these millennia later, and that bird-fish still busts me up. And could they *look* any more serious? They look like butlers on strike!

Ah. Good times.

Besides, if you aren't absolutely convinced that I'm the funniest God ever, then I've got exactly two words for you, pal.

Pope hat.

Thank you, thank you very much. I'll be here throughout eternity.

But to points: No, as a matter of fact, it is *not* enough that you "believe" in God. You've got to believe in *a* God. "God," as a concept, is automatically so vast and complex relative to its relationship to humans that it can't possibly do you or anyone else any real good unless it gets focused down to a specific context, or system. You can't have a relationship with a general idea. You need an actual *God* — one with a plan he's made known, and a history, and some sort of permanent, real identity you can interact with, and pray to, and consult. Otherwise, all you've got is something like a vague philosophy.

Of course, you're always free to just *start* a religion.

The problem with starting your own religion, though, is that it means you'll have to learn html coding, since these days starting a religion without having a really cool website for it is just wrong.

And do you really want to learn html coding?

I didn't think so.

So, ultimately, why Christianity, then?

Me, I thought you'd never ask.

Well, there are so many good reasons to Vote for Me that it's hard to know where to start. But here are just a few off the top of John's bald spot. (*John here! Not funny! God not hilarious!*)

* I came down there. Every other religion in the world involves you, way down where you are, and Le' Kahuna Grande, way up where he/she/it is. I'm the only God that came down to where you live — that, in fact, *became* one of you. That creates a means of intimacy — and establishes a depth of empathy — no one else even pretends to match.

* I had myself horribly murdered so that you would never have to bear the weight of your sins — or anyone else's. Talk about proving your love.

* I address guilt, *the* great human bugaboo. I give you a permanent, dependable, inexhaustible means of almost instantly cleansing yourself of Sin Karma. *No one*

but me has so clearly made it their singular business to help you sleep at night. It's either me or Sominex, Flippy.

* We're number one! We're number one!

* Life is hard. I make it easy. And I do it by giving _more_ of you to yourself, not less. Without me, you flip about in the wind: All you can do is react to the world, because you don't know who you are. With me, you're _so_ you that nothing, and nobody, can diminish you.

* I love you. You were created so that I could have a relationship with you. Which means I'm just going to keep knocking at your door until you invite me in. Don't think of me as God. Think of me as someone to whom your marriage was prearranged. And there's nothing you can do about it. Now c'mon. Help me pick out a china pattern.

* Becoming a Christian means inheriting a _massive_ support network. Christians are everywhere. And not the repressive, sin-fixated nut-job ones, either. Real ones. Humble people. Strong people. People it wouldn't kill you to know.

- Given how long eternity lasts, do you *really* want to gamble that Christianity is pure horse-pucky?

- And the last, but not least, reason I could think of right off the top of John's head for why you should become a Christian: Two thousand years, baby.

Two thousand years.

And the future's so bright, I gotta wear shades.

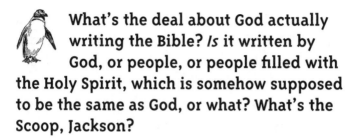 **What's the deal about God actually writing the Bible? _Is_ it written by God, or people, or people filled with the Holy Spirit, which is somehow supposed to be the same as God, or what? What's the Scoop, Jackson?**

Did you just call me "Jackson"?

"But the angel said to her, 'Do not be afraid, Mary, you have found favor with God. You will be with child and give birth to a son, and you are to give him the name Jackson.'"

"After six days Jackson took with him Peter, James, and John the brother of James, and led them up a high mountain by themselves. There he was transfigured before them. His face shone like the sun, and his clothes became as white as the light. Just then there appeared before them Moses and Elijah, talking with Jackson."

"For God so loved the world that he sent his only son, Jackson."

Yeah, that's not going to work for me.

Ah, it's good, though, to (almost) quote from and generally think about my first Good Book. What a keeper.

Of course, that book by me doesn't have what *this* one does, which is an Austin Powers joke.

But still — the *Bible!* Talk about a publishing sensation—before there even *was* publishing!

Ah. How I loved the ancient scribes of yore.

And let me tell you something: Yore was a tough place to work. Those Yorites were difficult people. Very cranky. Stuck in their ways.

No, but you gotta love the scribes. I sure do, anyway. You don't — at least not any more. Now you've got laser printers and inkjet printers and photo printers and Me knows what all to crank out your critical documents. Back in the day, though, I had a veritable army of *serious* artists dedicating all of their lives, talent, and training to drawing the perfect capital "A," or the Ultimate Comma, or whatever. It was awesome. I used to actually feel sorry for those guys, working by candlelight through the wee hours of the morning, sitting at their hard wooden desks on their hard wooden stools. That's why I blessed so many of them with giant backsides.

Which totally worked—except it tended to make local villagers suspicious that the scribes were secretly hoarding all the good food. "Then explain your huge butt!" they'd scream, brandishing their clubs and pitchforks. "Look at the can on ya! It's bigger than most of our hovels! Yer keepin' all the good food for yourself, ain't ya? You're in there suckin' down butter and pork fat, while we're out here chewin' on mud and bugs! Give it up, lard-ass! Bring out the good food!"

And all the poor scribe could say in response was, "Please, gentle folk, believe me when I say I have no idea how I came by my plenteous hindquarters! You all know my parents. You know there isn't enough fat between the two of them to make one decent baby's bottom. And look at the rest of me! If I was overeating, would I be so skinny everywhere else? Scribes simply grow monstrous rumps! We have no idea why! The only cause for it we can imagine is that God, in his infinite benevolence, bestows them upon us so that we can sit and transcribe his glorious Word for days on end, reveling in the wonder of his sweet, sacrificial Atonement for the ultimate salvation of us all!"

"Get him!" the peasants would scream, charging the scribe. Who would run away.

But never, ever fast enough.

And then things would just get ugly.

Boy. They don't call 'em the Dark Ages for nothing.

◆ ◆ ◆

Anyway, the Bible. That book is of two natures. The first is the *book* aspect of it — the part that involves manuscripts, and translations, and text that was written, identified, and settled upon over a very, very long time.

That part is essentially historical. It's fairly easy to deal with.

The other part of the Bible has to do with its mystical nature.

The idea behind the Bible, as you probably know, is that it was written by people who, while they were writing it, were filled with the Holy Spirit — in pretty much the same way I'm using John here. (*John here! Just call me Moses! Har! Kidding! Can barely part what's left of hair!*)

Which makes this as good a time as any to talk about the Holy Spirit.

In the Bible I actually _do_ talk about the Holy Spirit — and all the time, too. In John 14:13, for instance, I say, "...the Holy Spirit, whom the Father will send in my name, will teach you all things, and will remind you of everything I have said to you."

See? To all those who believed in me, I (God the Father) promised to send, via me (Jesus Christ), the Holy Spirit (me again!).

Killer plan, 'eh?

So many Westerners these days think the religions of the East have so much alluring, impenetrable mystery about them.

Please. You want impenetrable mystery? I've got your impenetrable mystery right here. I'm _three Gods in one!_

I'm the "Buy One, Get Two Free!" God!

How do I do it?

Actually, let's stop talking about the Holy Spirit for a moment, and make sure we're all clear on the Holy Trinity concept.

My world is created, defined, and expressed in three ...modes: the heavenly realm, the human realm, and you personally. From top to bottom, that's it. That's the whole enchilada.

Because I am God, it is in my nature to be at all times fully present in all three of these different aspects of what is (believe it or not!) one.

In heaven, I am the Father.

On (and within) life on earth, I am Jesus.

In you, I am the Holy Spirit.

And those three things are, in a very real sense, all jumbled together, making for One Big Thing.

It's all for (and in) one, and one for (and in) all, baby. That's the program.

It's a mystery (to you), for sure. Which means it's not *supposed* to fit into your normal brain. Some things — most of the *best* things, in fact — just don't. Even Christians don't claim to rationally understand the whole Triune Nature of God thing. The classic Christian statement on the matter, called the Athanasian Creed, reads, in part: "So the Father is God, the Son is God, and the Holy Ghost is God. And yet they are not three Gods, but one God. So likewise the Father is Lord, the Son is Lord, and the Holy Ghost is Lord. And yet they are not three Lords, but one Lord."

See? This is the only time and place in the universe where a person can confidently and legitimately assert that $1+1+1=1$.

People always think my purpose is to lay down rules.

When all along my real purpose has been to help you break through them all.

◆ ◆ ◆

The Holy Spirit, specifically, is all about this: I didn't want to become a man, arrive on earth, do my thing, and then just _leave_. Because I knew that if I did that, two generations after I returned here to heaven people back in the Holy Land would be saying stuff like, "Can you believe Grandpa thinks he actually saw _God_ walking around, as a regular _guy_, raising people from the dead and all that? Talk about senile. C'mon, we're gonna be late for the virgin sacrifice! I gotta see what Baal does when they try to pawn off on him Festus's sister, Heloise. If she's a virgin, I'm the Oracle of Delphi! Let's go!"

See? I'd be forgotten. I needed something that would really and permanently stick with people, something that would forever affect them the way they were first affected two thousand years ago — when, for instance, they saw me strolling around like the Duke of Earl three days after I'd been brutally murdered.

And I decided that that Ultimate Forget-Me-Not should be Me, in the form of the Holy Spirit.

The Holy Spirit is the means by which I become alive, personal, and immediate to people. It's that simple. Like I said before, you can't form a valid, constant relationship with a God who exists up in the sky somewhere while you're stuck down on earth. That's just not a workable arrangement. I want to be part of your life. I want to be where you are, feeling what you're feeling, doing what you're doing. I want to be right *there* for you, whenever, wherever, and however you want me to be. My imperative is to personalize my relationship with you in such a way as to leave you no doubt whatsoever that my entire purpose in existing at *all* is to be as clear as I can possibly be about how deeply and permanently I love you.

That would be you *personally*, Sport.

I take my role as Father very seriously.

The Holy Spirit is how I achieve my goal of continuous partnership with you; it's your individualized, internalized, *personalized* version of The Complete Me. And everybody has that — has me, fully delivered, fully available, all the time.

(I totally understand, by the way, what a stretch it is to imagine that All I Am is simultaneously inside every single human in the world. I know that can maybe seem a little *too* miraculous. But the truth is, it only seems like a miracle when you haven't experienced it. Once you've felt me, in Holy Spirit mode, come fully upon you, every question you might have about how that could work disappears. For now, just assume that I really *do* work in wonderful and mysterious ways. That's pretty much my whole thing. And think about it: Would you really want a God who simply finds it too *challenging* to do true miracles? Would that be good? Don't you want a God who's capable of doing things you can't even imagine? How thrilled would you be if you had to pray to your God like this: "Oh, benevolent Deity, who seems to have a pretty good grasp on things and is relatively powerful, are you busy just now? Because I don't want to intrude; I know how stressed out you get, with so many people praying to you at once. I sure hope this is an okay time, because I've got something I'd really like to ask you about. Is it possible you could arrange for us to have good weather in our area tomorrow night? I can draw you a map if you're not sure where I live. The thing is, I'm taking my date to the County Fair tomorrow night, and I really want things to go well. I think this could be the one! So nice, warm weather would be great. Now, God, I know that temperature and air pressure and all that are really difficult for you to control. I know it's just one of those things you're not too good at. But please, God, is there any possible way you could figure out how to handle weather before tomorrow night? I swear I'll put more money in the collection plate next time if you do. I mean, can you even do cloud control at this point? I sure do hope so, because I really want this date to go well. Anything you can manage to do about the weather would be great. If you don't think you can get it right, though, God, then please don't try at all, okay? I don't want a blizzard to hit, or a hurricane, or anything terrible like that. Just a plain, clear night would be best. Thanks for doing whatever you can manage, O Pretty Powerful One. We all know you're trying the best you can. That's all any of us can ask. Amen." See? What kind of God is that? Forget it. You want a God whose miracles _freak you out._)

And here's something that isn't often enough recognized, or put forth: I, as the Holy Spirit, come to you just as often if you're not a believer as I do if you are. It's just that if you're not a believer, you don't recognize me when I show up. But you intuit my presence, just the same. You might call it inspiration. You might call it Being At One With The Cosmos. You might call it getting high on life. You might even call it (for awhile, anyway) getting high, period. Whatever you call it, you sure as heck _know_ it when I come knocking on your door.

You feel me when you're in the forest. You feel me when you're at the ocean, or being dazzled by a sunset, or hearing music that particularly moves you.

That's _me,_ in those moments. That's my essence. When peace comes over you, or something wonderful happens to you, or everything just seems to be rolling your way for no reason you can think of — there I am.

I don't push myself on people. But I sure do everything I can to let them know I'm there.

I stay backstage, basically, and wait for them to deliver my cue.

You think oceans and forests are good for your soul? You think that special song really moves you?

Please.

Wait'll you meet me.

And with all my might I pray you understand that that moment, that singular, joyous moment in which you are filled with conscious, absolute knowledge of me via The Holy Ghost, is never more than one simple prayer away. (And that prayer, specifically, is whatever you need to say in order to bring us together. For starters, though, you can't do better than to use the short, glorious prayer Peter used when he felt so inspired by seeing me walk on water that he tried to do it himself — which he succeeded in doing, until he took his eyes off me, at which moment he burst out with something that *always* gets my full attention and response: "Lord, save me!")

Not to put too fine a point on it, but that moment is, in fact, exactly as far away as the distance between your knees and the floor.

The Bible, then, was written by people gripped in the ecstasy of the Holy Spirit. And that's why you need the Holy Spirit to read the thing, too.

The truth is that the Bible is so multifaceted, and so infused with the totality of my nature, and so miraculously (yes!) interconnected throughout all of its component parts, that in order to practically (let alone profoundly) understand it at all, you *must* have the Holy Spirit with you, or... or you'll put it down in five minutes, anyway. Trying to read the Bible without your Holy Spirit-brand spectacles on is like trying to drive a car with an empty gas tank. You just won't get very far.

If you're not a Christian, then for now just know this (which, since you're not a Christian, will sound stupid): The Bible was written for you. Its purpose is to connect your soul — your specific, individual, divinely unique soul — with mine. Period. That's it. It's exactly that personal. Other people have no business telling you what anything in the Bible means. Experts can help you understand such things about the Bible as its historical, geographical, and literary contexts — and anyone trying to get through the book really should seek out that kind of informed expertise. But when it comes to the Bible's mystical essence — to the part where the Me in heaven is using it to talk to the Me in you — trust that you'll know what things in it *mean* when you and I read it together. Before then, screw what anybody else says I *meant* when I said this or did that in the Bible.

People (as you know, I know) are forever using the Bible to support all kinds of whacked-out delusions and agendas. Some crankcase could decide that everyone in the world should live with a wine cork jammed up their left nostril — and as sure as I can make the sun rise on time tomorrow morning he'll have a Bible quote to support his position. That stuff drives me crazy. I can't even begin to tell you how exhausted I am with people pushing their own fears and hatred into my mouth. I don't care how legitimate or "accepted" the hyper-groomed Christian Network TV news anchor might seem to you: If, in my name, he's condemning, or blaming, or just _kvetch-ing_ in the manner so many Christians tend to, please assume that he's no more speaking for me than anything you'd get out of a little rubber ducky you'd squeeze in the bathtub.

When I want you to hear my message, I guarantee that you will.

And when you _do_ hear it, you're very likely to be awed at what a simple message it is. I don't see how it could really be any simpler. When, in the New Testament, I'm asked to boil down to the bare bone everything I've ever taught throughout the centuries, I answer, "Sure, you funky Pharisees. It all boils down to: Love me with all of your heart, and love your neighbor as you love yourself. So is there any dip for these chips, or what?"

Okay, I didn't say the chips part. Or "funky Pharisees."

Not as far as _you_ know, anyway.

But I sure did say that the rest of it (at Matthew 22:37). And I sure did mean it.

Love me with all of your heart, and love your neighbor as you love yourself. (Within the Christian tradition, by the way, those words are known as the "Great Commandment.")

That, mis amigos, is the whole Bible — in twenty words or less.

The rest of the book is just... well, you can save that for later. First things first, and all that.

Even if I do believe in Christ, do I really have to go to church every Sunday? Yuck.

Yes. You have to. Those are the rules. If you want to be a Christian then you have to go to church every single Sunday morning for the rest of your life. If in any given year you miss more than four Sundays, I'm afraid I'll then have no choice but to smote you forthrightly.

Or at least let the air out of one of your car tires. Or maybe bust out the bottom of a grocery bag you're carrying. Make sure you have three bad hair days in a row. Something.

Oh, I'll do it, baby! Don't think I won't. Because _I will!_

No — of course you don't have to go to church. No one _has_ to do much of anything. But the reason so many people keep _choosing_ to go to church is as simple as it gets: They know that they can't have a relationship with me if they don't ever come over to my house. It's just that simple. Church _is_ my home, you know; that really _is_ where I hang out. You get hints and intimations of me in your everyday life, for sure — but at church you get a huge honkin' *helping* of me. Maximum exposure. Major bang for your buck.

I go where people pray, see? And a lot of people do a lot of praying at church.

I'm in the wood at church. I'm in the carpet. I'm in the pews. I'm in the *air* there, Care Bear.

Got to go where the action is, right?

Also, being a Christian has some aspects to it that are a real challenge to maintain. Mostly, it's hard to remember that you find your richest pleasure in doing my will, not yours. And it's *really* hard to remember that right after you've had your typical Friday and Saturday night — not to mention that all-consuming work week.

Actually, I'm almost surprised when *anyone* shows up for church.

Almost.

People show up for church because they want — because they know they *need* — the support they find there. It's just plain good to pray with others. You get a hundred people in a room silently bowing their heads and communing with me, and you've got yourself one amazing moment. There's just nothing else in the world like it.

Plus, in regular life, people tend to be...how should I put this...freakin' _obnoxious,_ right? They drive you crazy. They're stupid, frustrating, stubborn, lazy, and so blatantly insane that it counts as one of the greatest mysteries of life that they can even dress themselves in the morning, much less show up for work every day to further their unstoppable efforts to systematically destroy everything in your life that they possibly can.

Okay? That's people. You can't live with them, and you can't figure out a way to dispose of their bodies without getting caught.

Me, that's awful. But you know what I mean. People are just extremely difficult to coexist with.

But not in church!

You know what church does? It turns people from pessimists to optimists. Because at church, everyone you see—from the greeter at the door to the person up front leading the whole thing—is your partner. Your friend.

Your fellow angel.

Because believe this: At church, everyone's a saint.

At church, you look at someone, and you see that gleam in their eye, and it's Me. And they see that gleam in your eye, and it's Me. And they know it, and you know it, and everyone shaking hands or exchanging greetings knows it, and before any of you know it, you're all bashfully rejoicing at the joy of my presence in and among you all: You feel like you're at the greatest, classiest party of your life, one being held in honor of the world, and everything in it that's good.

And I, of course, am that party's Heavenly Host.

Every Sunday, y'all.

And here you thought church was boring. Would *that* many people volunteer to go be bored every Sunday morning? Do you think you have a *lower* tolerance for boredom than everybody else?

Well, you don't, Sparky.

Listen, people don't go to church because they're spiritual robots, programmed to do the same thing at the same time every Sunday. People go to church because they, like everyone else in the world, are naturally drawn to go wherever they can find the most love.

Here's the thing, too, about going to church: You've *really* got to find the right church for you. Finding the right church is every bit like finding the love of your life: It just broadsides you with its...rightness.

And if it doesn't, then it's not.

In other words, if you're wondering whether the church you're going to is the right one for you, it's not. Some are very liberal. Some are very conservative. Traditional, modern, small, large, active, passive—there are as many kinds of churches as there are people. Trust this: You'll know the right church for _you_ when you find it. Sooner or later you're going to be at a service, and it's going to feel so good, and so right, that you're going to want to cry.

And there's your new church.

And going there the following Sunday will feel as natural as eating when you're hungry, and drinking when you're thirsty.

So how would being a Christian actually improve my life? What would it really *do* for me?

Oh, my, how my Answer Cup is already runnething over.

It's making quite the mess, too. Sticky, clingy, tacky, gluey, gummy, and even viscid adjectives are spilling everywhere. And I'll be cleaning, scrubbing, wiping, swabbing, shampooing, brushing, and banishing verb stains from the rug for days.

Well, maybe not *banishing* them anywhere. But you know what I'm saying.

Speaking of me not saying another word, isn't asking me how becoming a Christian would improve your life a bit like asking a travel agent how going on a cruise would relax you? Wouldn't it be better to ask people who have actually *been* on a cruise what it did or didn't do for them? You betcha.

So here's an idea. Let's ask John — the John whose mind and body I'm sharing in order to write this book — what becoming a Christian has done for him. I'll pull back now, and let him tell you what being with me has done for his life. Go ahead, John.

Hilo! Jhon is here! Howw are you? Howz the weather where you are be? Is it rain or cold? Hope no! I am live in San Diego, where the warm is mostly here. Good! Even at Christmas when cold is not here we are too hot to eat but a lot. I am happy. I have a cat. The tail of it bends wrong at end. No hurting it, but! A kinky cat! Actuallee true! Had dog once, and cat, which was wrong, sneeked up to it from behind, and

God here again.

Okay, that didn't work out.

I swear: That guy thinks he is just sooooo funny.

See how funny he thinks it is when he wakes up one morning with an ear growing out of the middle of his forehead.

Okay, well, listen: What asking me into your life will do for you is to (gradually, over time, at a rate that is always comfortable for you) eradicate fear from your heart and mind.

In that sense, I really am the Ultimate One Trick Pony.

But what a trick!

I am the Fear Eliminator.

Here's a fact: You have no idea how afraid you are, or of what that fear has done to your life. You fear at such a deep, fundamental level that it affects, if not completely dominates, every moment of your life. You aren't aware of it in the way you aren't aware of your blood: It's just how you live.

You were *designed* to fear. You *must* fear.

What, after all, *isn't* frightening about the human experience?

Being born: Completely terrifying. Forced out of the only warm, nurturing place you've ever known. Bright lights. Jarring noises. Completely Alien Universe. Circumcision, maybe — and *that's* if you're lucky enough to be born male.

Living: Sheer terror. Could die any minute. Total lack of control.

Dying: Enough said.

Okay? All that is really frightening.

Mainly, it's the Being Out of Control thing. You are out of control of your life, and you know it — and when that fact isn't driving you nuts, it's terrifying you. You don't know what's going to happen to you tomorrow — or in the next four seconds. And you don't know why things happened to you in the past, either.

Worst of all, by far, is that you have no idea what's going to happen to you after you die.

You operate atop this undulating, trembling foundation of fear — this haunting, abiding conviction that it doesn't really matter what you do, say, or think, because ultimately you're just going to _die_ anyway.

And that's so scary — since you have no idea what that actually means. And that singular fear naturally sprouts out into all _kinds_ of fears and anxieties and weirdness.

Becoming a Christian eradicates all of those fears and concerns. And it doesn't do it by making you _stupid_, either: I know it can seem that way to a nonbeliever. What Christianity does do is _fit_ you. It turns you into the you that you can't be without it, because it is _the_ piece of your puzzle that you're missing.

Oh, and it brings you the sure knowledge that you're going to live forever.

So. How do _you_ spell relief?

113

I was as serious as serious gets when I said that I made you in my image. And the best you can do without me is to strive to create yourself in *your* image. On your own, all you can do is frantically try to control your own world, to run things your own way, to be master of your own fate.

And then wonder, every single night when you're trying to fall asleep, why in the world it isn't working.

I can't tell you all the ways becoming a Christian would improve your life. Only you can. Only you know what in your life most needs changing.

All I can promise you is that, with me, you'll overcome any and all obstacles standing between you and peace.

Why would you choose to continue struggling as a human, when divinity is so clearly, and so constantly, calling you?

AFTERWORD
by John Shore

Hi. John Shore here. Sorry about that I'm a Burbling Moron joke before. It was funny—but wrong. Anyway, I thought you might like to know what my personal deal is with Christianity. It's kind of interesting, maybe, in that the split-second before I very suddenly and all at once became a Christian (um, for the record I'd like to say that, as far as I can tell, God suddenly converts people who have proven themselves too dense to get it any other way), I couldn't possibly have been *less* of a Christian. If anything, I was *anti*-Christian. The religion struck me as ridiculously immature, a way-too-obvious system designed mostly to capitalize on people's guilt: Big Daddy in the Sky knows you did wrong, but will love you anyway if you'll only admit that he's perfection itself, and that you're a wretched, sickening sack of sin.

Please. I always figured that if I wanted Father Knows Best, I'd watch TV.

And it wasn't like I didn't believe in anything. I did. I very seriously believed in me. I hadn't a doubt in the world but that I was somebody truly worthy of my utmost affection and devotion. I was strong, capable, friendly, competent — I was just a general, all-around good guy. I was thirty-eight years old. I'd been happily married for fifteen years. I had a good job. I had friends. People liked me. *I* liked me.

That is, I liked myself as much as it seemed reasonable to do so. I was certainly not unaware of my own short-comings (which I won't share with you here, in order to save my friends and former friends the shock of suddenly realizing what happened, that one time, to their stashes of porno and pot). But I didn't need God or anybody else to forgive me for the times I behaved poorly. I was per-fectly capable (if not spectacularly efficient) at forgiving myself, thank you very much.

Because I knew that, at my core, I was a good, morally sound person.

On the other hand, I was a human being. And human beings, I knew (boy, did I know) have natural needs, and natural weaknesses.

The paramount imperative, I believed, was to love myself. That's what it was all about: loving, and forgiving, oneself. Those who mastered that, mastered life. You had to be your own parents, your own nurturer, your own best friend.

Who could argue with that?

Then one day I was sitting at my desk at work during a totally typical weekday, feeling regretful about a particularly immature, semi-destructive thing I'd recently done, when this feeling started coming over me that in about four seconds had my undivided attention.

"What the hell?" I thought—and the next thing I knew I was very nearly desperate to be alone somewhere. It felt like warm water was filling me up inside—but downward, starting at just beneath my scalp. Right about when the "water" had moved from my neck to my chest I knew that whatever was happening to me wasn't going to stop.

117

And I could tell it was something spiritual, or psychological — or something basically non-physical.

"I'll be right back," I said to a co-worker — and then cut out for an auxiliary supply closet in our office no one ever used. I flipped on its light, closed its door behind me, and waited.

I closed my eyes. The intensity of what was happening made that seem like a good idea.

And what happened, rather all at once, was that I saw what an *asshole* I was. Isn't that awful? All at once, the truth was before me that instead of being a good guy who's basically always trying to do the right thing, I was a selfish, emotional weakling who was always doing and saying whatever best served my own needs at the time.

I never lied; but I'd fudge the truth here and there if it didn't really hurt anybody and would help things roll my way.

I never cheated; but life is complex, and sometimes one has to make deals that more directly serve a Larger Good.

I wanted to help others; but there were so many good shows on TV, especially after a long, rough day at work.

What suddenly became a fact to me was that I'd been fooling myself for so long I'd forgotten the act. I wasn't the great, honorable person I started out to be, that I'd meant to become — that I actually thought I _was_. I was just another guy so busy thinking he's constructing the perfect home that he doesn't realize how long ago he stopped using a level.

Man, I hate it when that happens.

I hate it when my whole view of myself is suddenly deconstructed and replaced by a view of myself that is _so_ not what I expected.

I hate it when in one second I go from being Batman to being the Penguin.

Actually, though, that wasn't the worst part. By far.

The worst part was that, accompanying that Less Than Peachy view of myself, was the very real knowledge that it was never, ever, _ever_ going to change.

Ever. Never. Ever.

I was born as I was. I had spent my life as I was. And I would die as I'd always been: small, selfish, and mean as a pissed-off penguin.

And there was absolutely nothing I could do about it.

I'd already spent my whole life trying to. Miserable mediocrity was the *best* I could do. I could achieve *that* only when I'd somehow pulled it together enough not to be a completely craven animal.

On a *good* day I was the Penguin!

And then here's what happened: I saw my death. I mean, I didn't see myself, like, writhing around after I'd been hit by a truck on the freeway or anything—I didn't see *how* I would die. But I did see, in a sort of direct, open tunnel, the disturbingly short distance between where I was and where I was most certainly going. I saw my mortality. I saw the simple fact that I *would* die—and that, as surely as one day follows the next, at the moment of my death I wouldn't be any different than I'd been at any other moment of my life.

I wasn't going to get better. I wasn't going to become stronger, or cleaner, or wiser, or smarter, or more honorable. It just wasn't going to happen. I was thirty-eight. I was who I'd die being. At *best*.

Oh, but that was a bad, bad moment for me. I can't even guess at what the *second* most terrible moment of my life is. Whatever it is, it's a very distant second.

It was at this point that I experienced yet another won-derful What-the-Hell-Is-Happening-to-Me? moment: My legs disappeared from underneath me. Gone. Buckled. Folded. Kaput with the leg support. Hello, hard ground, foundation of human existence, it's nice to see you, I'm surprised we don't get together more often, have you met my knees? It had happened to me once before: When I was twelve and had just come home after yet another fab-ulous Little League game, my father informed me that my mother, whom I hadn't in any way seen or heard from in two years, had returned and wanted to have lunch with me — and hey, whaddaya know! — my legs were gone. At that time, sinking to the floor, I had no thought more complicated or intense than, "My legs have stopped working."

Twenty-six years later, I found myself again thinking, "My legs have stopped working."

And then, sure enough, I was on my knees.

In the supply closet.

At my job.

Looking at my miserable, weak future, straight to my miserable, means-nothing death. It was just me and the cold, hard, gray, flat fact of...me. Which was never going to change. I just did not have the will or means or character to change who I was, which was exactly who I'd always been.

I saw that my life, in any way that could possibly matter, was over.

I then began doing something that, for me, made falling to my knees look like something I did every eight seconds. I started to cry.

Because isn't the whole point of being alive to be someone you'd really *want* to be?

If not, then what is *People* magazine *for?*

Anyway, I'm down and out. Right? You with me?

For your sake, I (almost) hope not.

So I'm kneeling there, blinded by my sad, stupid little fate, when, from up and off to my left, I hear a disembodied voice say something.

And it says what it says in a clear, distinct cartoon voice.

Listen, I grew up glued to cartoons. As a kid, I had absolutely no idea what was happening with adults, who were clearly insane. But Daffy Duck, I got. Porky Pig was my kind of guy. Wiley Coyote? Please — my very alter-ego!

To this day, I practically shiver with joy when _The Simpsons_ are on.

Anyway, of course I can't exactly describe the cartoon voice I heard. But, you know: goofy, precise, rich, psuedo-edgy. Cartoonish.

And what that voice said, from up and off to my left somewhere — from offstage — was, "Isn't this what Jesus is for?"

And just like that, I stopped crying.

And do you know what I knew at that moment — what instantly _imprinted_ itself upon me? That the story of Jesus is historically true. That it happened. That God, desiring above all else to show the people he'd created that he loved them, became a human, and came to earth, and sacrificed himself, and in every way did every thing he possibly could to show people exactly how deeply and terribly he loves them.

That's what my conversion consisted of: a sudden, sure knowledge that the historical story of Christ is true.

It wasn't, like, *wisdom* at all. I wasn't suddenly filled with the Mind of God, or anything like that. My soul didn't light up. Angels didn't sing for me. Nothing like that happened. In a way, it was about as boring as learning the year house paint was invented, or that your bank has slightly altered its Saturday hours. All that had changed was that I was now *sure* that the story of Christ, about which I had always scoffed if I ever thought of it at all, was true.

Then it was like how, when it starts to rain, you think about the only thing you *can* think, which is: "Oh. Now everything will get wet."

That's about what I thought: "Oh. Now I'm a Christian."

So I stood, wiped my eyes, opened the door to the supply closet, and went back to work.

And that was that.

◆ ◆ ◆

My Supply Closet conversion happened, as I write this, eight years ago. Between now and then I can honestly say that every single aspect of my life has improved to a degree that makes me grateful for the Christian context in which to understand it, since otherwise I guess I'd just think I went bonkers (or, at the very least, gotten some *extremely* good therapy). Never, ever in my wildest dreams did I imagine that life could be so...good. So pleasing. So delightful.

Well, I see that somewhere along the line I've become a walking Hallmark Card. How sweet of me.

"Find Me: Lose Your Personality." Now *there's* a Christian bumper sticker. Instead of a fish, I'm gonna put a little metal $\varnothing$ on my car. (Actually, one of the core things I was most surprised to discover about Christianity was how wrong my long-held assumption had been that in a very real way the whole point of the religion was to turn everybody into identical Church Drones. Wrong, wronger, wrongest. It is, instead, all about God helping each person turn into *Super Whoever They Are!*)

The main way becoming a Christian has changed my life is that now I'm "just" a happier, nicer person than I used to be. I used to be a lot harsher to people, particularly in how I thought about them. I'm Beyond Amazed to say that today I have a lot more patience with people: I'm more empathetic, I more closely identify with whatever they're feeling and thinking. I used to judge more; now I listen more. If God loved me enough to come swooping in and save my sorry butt, the least I can do is listen sympathetically when someone — when *anyone* — is talking to me, and to show that person respect. No problem.

I'm also a lot easier on myself. I used to be *really* harsh on myself. Now I'm less so. Again, if God loves me, who am I to question God's judgment? It makes me feel like I must be all right after all.

Anyway, stuff like that. I'm just a happier, nicer, calmer, more dependable, more *moral* guy than I used to be. Which, I know, sounds like bragging. Which is funny, because the whole thing about being a Christian is that it's so awesomely humbling that it's all you can do to not, like, spend all your time on your knees. It makes you feel the *opposite* of proud. I used to think I sometimes did bad things; now I know that doing bad things is at the core of my entire identity. It's in my nature. I was *born* to be selfish, arrogant, vain, dishonest, impatient, lazy, and greedy.

And Sleepy. And Grumpy. And Dopey. And Horny.

Man. Especially horny.

Well, that'll be another book.

The point is: What I learned in the supply closet is that I, alone, would never, ever be able to change or really even affect any of the negative things about myself.

And *that*, as it turns out, is precisely what Jesus is for.

ACKNOWLEDGMENTS

For their wonderful help and encouragement I'm deeply indebted to: Deborah Schneider, my discoverer Charlie Schneider, acquirer extraordinaire Lucas Smith, Kim Cohn, Jan Dennis, Richard Lederer, Richard Louv, Jackie Mitchard, Greg Johnson, Kim Flachmann, Michael Flachmann, Wes Yoder, Eric Metaxas, Scott Richardson, Matthew Paul Turner, Burt and Barb Person, Larry and Roz Duthie, Patricia Davis, Steve Kissing, John Penrose, Jenna Peterson, Allen Randall, Deborah Baldwin, Catt Fields, Barry Finnegan, Jackie Hammel, Rick Hornor, Jessica Kruskamp, Carl Nelson, Delle Willett, Jaime Windon, John Eagleson, and Liana MacKinnon.